PLANES, NAMES

NOSE ART SERIES

& *Dames*

VOL. II
1946-1960

by Larry Davis
Illustrated by Don Greer

squadron/signal publications

(Cover)
LT James Thompson flew *THE HUFF*. The dragon motif symbolized the MiG-15 that Thompson shot down on 18 May 1953, which had a large dragon painted on the fuselage.

(Overleaf)
SNUGGLEBUNNY was a B-29A of the 98th Bomb Group (Medium) on the PSP ramp at Yokota Air Base, Japan during 1951. *SNUGGLEBUNNY* flew a total of 140 combat missions, sixty-five during the Second World War and seventy-five in Korea. (USAF)

Maximum Goose and *Minimum Goose*, a pair of 412th Fighter Group P-80A Shooting Stars, share the ramp at the Washington National Airport during the Army Air Force Air Show held in May of 1946. (USAF)

If you have any photographs of the aircraft, armor, soldiers or ships of any nation, particularly wartime snapshots, why not share them with us and help make Squadron/Signal's books all the more interesting and complete in the future. Any photographs sent to us will be copied and the original returned. The donor will be fully credited for any photos used. Please send them to:

Squadron/Signal Publications, Inc.
1115 Crowley Drive
Carrollton, TX 75011-5010

Acknowledgements

Air Force Museum	John Andrews
Tom Brewer	Harvey Brown
John Campbell	Bill Cleveland
Bill Coffey	Don Dickman
Karl Dittmer	Bob Esposito
Jeff Ethell	Jim Farmer
V. A. Fleming	Tom Foote
Don Garrett, Jr.	Dick Geiger
Larry Hendel	John Horne
Marty Isham	Robert Jackson
Keith Johnson	Dick Kempthorne
Bernard Kibort	Robert Lamprecht
George Lovering	Ernie McDowell
Dave McLaren	David W. Menard
Joe Michaels	Barry Miller
Robert C. Mikesh	Mosquito Association
Tom Mullen	North American Aviation
Merle Olmsted	Ron Picciani
William Ritchie	Bill Ritter
Dick Starinchak	John Shipley
Jim Sullivan	Norm Taylor
Warren Thompson	Frank Tomlinson
U.S. Air Force	Paul Vercammen

Introduction

Nose art — there is no definition for it in any Webster's Dictionary, but just ask any air or ground crewmen from any war since the Second World War and they'll tell you not only what it is, but what it meant to them. It was a way of personalizing a piece of machinery that you had to depend on and it appeared on almost everything that was used in combat, from aircraft to tanks. Most of the really beautiful and/or outrageous art appeared on aircraft.

In the Second World War, nose art was divided into four basic categories: home, patriotism or the war, music and sex. Aircraft were named after pieces of that far away, lost item — home. "Bainbridge Belle" and "Jersey Jerk" were examples of this. Patriotism and the war caused many a flourish with the paint brush. Hitler and Tojo were often seen being battered about on the sides of B-17s and B-24s. The music of World War 2 also led to a great many names like "Pistol Packin' Mama" which was used on almost every fighting aircraft type in the war.

But undoubtedly, it was the magical three letter word SEX that led to most of the art work. Naked and almost naked women were painted on every type of aircraft, in almost every air force. Some of it was beautifully done like "Cherokee Strip" and "Sugar Puss." Some of it quite vulgar, such as the 8th Air Force B-17s "Mount 'N Ride" or "Rosie's Sweat Box." Quite a bit of the nose art was copied from Vargas paintings that appeared in Esquire magazine, the World War 2 equivalent to Playboy. The Vargas girls were never named in the magazine but carried every conceivable name when repeated on the aircraft. Nose art became so popular that many times the aircraft name and art was also painted on the crews flight jackets, especially in the 8th Air Force.

But when war broke out in Korea, the American public, the GIs and the professional soldiers were all a little confused. Very few people knew why we were in Korea in the first place. Consequently, the nose art reflected this confusion. Oh sure, there still was the ever present subject of SEX and this was quite apparent on the B-29s that took the war deep into North Korea. The 19th BOMB GROUP based at Kadena was even subjected to censorship on their aircraft. It seems that the base commander at Kadena had his wife living with him on base, and she got upset at seeing all that nudity on the nose of the aircraft. Never mind that the crews were laying their lives on the line each and every day, against a very formidable foe. She put the pressure on her husband and he ordered that all nose art be "clothed." And so

it was that beautiful art work like LT Dick Thompson's "That's It" had panties and bra painted on.

But there was something lacking with the feelings of the GIs that were fighting the war — and it showed in the nose art. The attitude toward the communists showed with names like "Red Eraser" and "United Notions." But most of the time it took the form of names like "Purple Shaft" and "Beat Up Bastard." The musical side of the nose art equation also wasn't there. The song titles reminded everyone that they really didn't want to be there, so very few aircraft were named after songs. Frankie Laine's "Mule Train" and Rosemary Clooney's "Come On 'A My House" being exceptions. Much of the fighter nose art was captured from feelings towards the aircraft they flew. "Mach One Mac," "MiG Mad Marine" and "Gopher Patrol" being good examples of Sabre nose art.

Art work on stateside units, when it was allowed, was more along the lines of the Second World War. Perhaps it was the pride of the stateside crews showing, not that the air and ground crews in Korea had a lack of pride — far from it. Pride was almost the only thing that got the crews through what amounted to the worst fighting conditions since Valley Forge. There just wasn't anything easy about the Korea War, except dying. Back in the states, the air and ground crews decorated aircraft for the many non-combat tests. They called them "competitions." The Air Force World Wide Rocket Meet held at Yuma AFB prior to the William Tell Meets was a fine example. Only the best units were sent to Yuma. Special teams were selected, not only from a group or wing, but many times from an air division that would have up to six or seven squadrons. And these crews would apply nose art to the aircraft that were selected to hold up the honor of their unit. The 498th Fighter Interceptor Squadron, known as the "Geiger Tigers," had all their aircraft named and carried nose art for the 1956 Yuma Meet. Even Strategic Air Command bombing competitions saw a little use of nose art, although I'm sure that GEN Curtis LeMay frowned upon it.

With the exception of the friendly competitions held throughout the world in the late 1950s and early 1960s, nose art simply faded away. A few units had aircraft that were named, like the 538th Fighter Interceptor Squadron's F-104As, but nothing gaudy, or patriotic and especially not sexy! It would remain for another little war in another far off little country for the nose art fad to make a return. The country was South Vietnam and the war would last over seven years!

SWEET MUSIC, a P-47D Thunderbolt of the 508th Fighter Squadron/404th Fighter Group based at Fritzlar Airdrome, Germany after the end of WWII, carries the group insignia on the cowling in addition to its musical "art." (Jeff Ethell)

3

The *FLYING SHAMROCK* was a P-47M Thunderbolt of the 456th Fighter Squadron/414th Fighter Group based at North Field, Iwo Jima during late 1945. (George Lovering)

R.O.N., an abbreviation for official orders calling for the crew to Remain Over Night. The A-26C Invader was assigned to the Ohio Air National Guard. (David W. Menard)

An unnamed but certainly colorful P-47D Thunderbolt of the 397th Fighter Squadron/368th Fighter Group based at Straubling, Germany after the war. The Black and Yellow bands around the rear fuselage were used to identify aircraft assigned to the German Occupation Forces. (Jeff Ethell)

This Consolidated B-24J Liberator based at Nome, Alaska during 1947 carries a highly unique form of the classic sharkmouth design. (AFM)

Many Second World War units kept their wartime markings long after the war ended, as did *WHAT'S UP DOC!*, an F-51D Mustang of the 35th Fighter Group based at Irumagawa Air Base, Japan during 1949. (Bob Pattison)

This P-47D Thunderbolt named *Slick Chick* was the personal aircraft of the group commander of the 368th Fighter Group, COL Frank Perego. (Jeff Ethell)

The First Lady, Mamie Eisenhower, christens the C-121 Presidential aircraft (today known as Air Force One) on 24 November 1954. President Eisenhower's aircraft was named *Columbine III*. (AFM)

BUG'S BUCKET O' BOLTS was a P-80A with the 412th Fighter Group at March Field, California during 1946. The 412th Fighter Group was the first operational unit to be equipped with the Lockheed P-80 Shooting Star. (USAF)

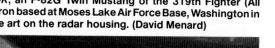

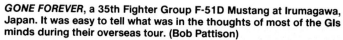

SPOKANE SPOOK, an F-82G Twin Mustang of the 319th Fighter (All Weather) Squadron based at Moses Lake Air Force Base, Washington in 1949, carried the art on the radar housing. (David Menard)

GONE FOREVER, a 35th Fighter Group F-51D Mustang at Irumagawa, Japan. It was easy to tell what was in the thoughts of most of the GIs minds during their overseas tour. (Bob Pattison)

Many of the A-26C Invaders of the Michigan Air Guard carried names and/or nose art similar to *BIG DEAL*. This Invader was the wing commander's aircraft. (David W. Menard)

THE DUCHESS was another 35th Fighter Group F-51D Mustang based at Irumagawa, Japan that retained its Second World War nose art. (Bob Pattison)

Ready For Freddie was another F-51D Mustang of the Irumagawa-based 35th Fighter Group during 1949. Most of the group's Mustangs had nose art of some sort. (Bob Pattison)

This P-61A Black Widow night-fighter of the 52nd Fighter (All Weather) Group has had its top turret removed, prompting the crew to name the aircraft FLAT TOP. (Dave McLaren)

Rhapsody In Rivets was flown by COL Bruce Holloway, Commander of the 412th Fighter Group at March Field, California. The multi-colored bands around the rear fuselage are command bands. (USAF)

"Reddi Kilowatt" adorns the engine nacelles of this Lockheed F-5G Lightning named I'M REDDI. The aircraft was operated by the Weather Modification Company. (W.J. Balogh)

The *Big Stud* was Bob Baseler's P-47N Thunderbolt. The aircraft was used to advertise for Army Air Force recruiters at air shows during 1946. (W. J. Balogh)

The *TEXAS TAILPIPE*, F-86A (49-1028) of the 56th Fighter Group, was flown by COL Robert Casey when the group was based at Orchard Place AFB (now Chicago's O'Hare Airport) during the early 1950s. (USAF)

7

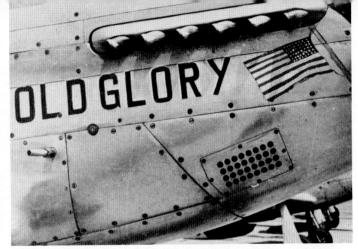

Old Glory adorned the nose of this 40th Fighter Squadron/35th Fighter Group F-51D Mustang based in Japan during early 1950. (Bob Pattison)

The *HURRICANE HUNTERS* carried the patch of the 53rd STRATEGIC RECONNAISSANCE SQUADRON on the nose of their Superforts when they were based at Kindley Air Force Base in Bermuda. (AFM)

The Davey Crockett was a Douglas C-54 flown by the Continental Air Division of the Military Air Transport Service (MATS) during 1947. (USAF)

Baby Jean and the rest of the 412th Fighter Group's P-80As on the ramp at Washington National Airport during 1946. Each pilot's Second World War score is carried on the vertical fin. "Jean" was the Deputy Group Commander's aircraft. (USAF)

NIGHT 'TAKEOFF,' an F-82G Twin Mustang of the 319th Fighter (All Weather) Squadron at Moses Lake Air Force Base, Washington. Most of the Twin Mustang interceptors from the 319th carried art of some type on the radar housing. (David Menard)

Some of the art work on the F-51D Mustangs of the 40th Fighter Squadron reflected the pilot's previous Second World War service. The pilot of DESERT RAT had served with the 57th Fighter Group in North Africa. (Bob Pattison)

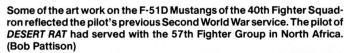

THE BIG WHEEL, an Army Ryan L-17B Navion, was the personal aircraft used by the commander of 8th U.S. Army in Korea. The aircraft was based at Yokota Air Base, Japan during 1949. (Fred LePage)

9

MAGGIE was a C-119C that was also named *TEXAS ROSE* when she was assigned to the 64th Troop Carrier Squadron, the Blue Tailed Flies. "Maggie" was based at Pusan during the Fall of 1952. (Robert C. Mikesh)

CHIEF SPOKANE was *THE RED ERASER*, an indication of the destructive power of a full load of bombs from this B-29A Superfortress of the 92nd Bomb Group. (AFM)

SCAP stood for Supreme Commander Allied Powers. This was GEN Douglas MacArthur's personal C-121 on the ramp at Kimpo soon after the airfield was retaken following the Inchon landings in September of 1950. (Army)

ATOMIC TOM was one of the first B-29s to see combat in the Korean War, flying on the first 19th Bomb Group mission of the war (26 June 1950). (Bill Ritter)

CAPT. SAM AND TEN 'SCENTS' described the aroma of the crew after sweating out any mission that took them into MiG Alley in northwest Korea. (Hill)

SAC MATE, was a play on the Strategic Air Command title of the B-29 force in Korea. This 22nd Bomb Group (M) B-29A was based at Kadena in the Fall of 1950. (Tom Brewer)

Many times the names and/or art work were changed when crews changed. *T.D.Y. WIDOW* changed 98th Bomb Group (Medium) crews during 1952 and while the new crew liked the name, they wanted a different lady. (AFM)

When they took over the aircraft, the new crew of *T.D.Y. WIDOW* added an entirely new female "mascot" to the nose of the B-29A Superfortress. (AFM)

11

MOON'S MOONBEAM was an RB-29A of the 91st Strategic Reconnaissance Squadron at Yokota AB, Japan during 1951. She was later renamed *Daijobu* and flew long range reconnaissance missions along both the Red Chinese and Soviet borders during the Korean War. (Tom Mullen)

HOT TO TROT was C-119C Flying Boxcar of the 50th Troop Carrier Squadron at Johnson Air Base, Japan during 1950. (Bob Pattison)

Even these TARZON radio-controlled 12,000 pound bombs carried nose art. TARZON bombs were directed to their targets, usually the North Korean bridges across the Yalu River, from 19th Bomb Group B-29 "mother ships." (AFM)

A very scantily clad Indian maiden graced the nose of this 19th Bomb Group B-29A Superfortress named *APACHE*. (AFM)

COLONEL BRADY'S DIXIE Special was a 3rd Bomb Wing (Light) B-26C Invader that flew some of the dangerous anti-radar missions, now known as WILD WEASEL missions, when it was based at Kunsan, Korea during 1952. (John Horne)

THE BIG GASS BIRD was a 98th Bomb Group (Medium) B-29A Superfortress based at Yokota Air Base, Japan during 1952. (AFM)

An unnamed nude adorns the nose of this 13th Bomb Squadron/3rd Bomb Group (L) B-26B Invader based at Kunsan, Korea in 1952. The eight fixed forward firing .50 caliber machine guns on the B-26B made it a great attack aircraft. (John Horne)

The name Wrights Delight's/They Chose'n Flew was an obvious reference by the crew of this B-29A Superfortress to the area of Korea (Chosen) that their missions were flown against. (AFM)

HEAVENLY LADEN, a B-29A from the 98th Bomb Group (M), carries the Black undersurfaces called for when the MiG-15s made daylight missions into North Korea impossible for the B-29 force to continue, even with F-86 fighter cover. (USAF)

CHOTTO MATTE, a B-29A from the 98th Bomb Group(M), being refueled at Yokota for another strike against communist targets in North Korea in December of 1951. The B-29s used SHORAN radar to get a fix on their blacked out targets during their night missions. (Army)

The *LEMON DROP KID* was a 19th Bomb Group B-29A Superfortress that was named after a Bob Hope movie character and came complete with a cartoon character of the famous actor. (John Senior)

A mechanic checks the engines of *Dark Eyes*, an RB-26C from the 12th TRS/67th TRW at Kimpo during July 1951 as an M16 anti-aircraft halftrack moves by. The RB-26C had flown at least 108 missions over Korea. (USAF)

LT Johnston stands next to his *FAT CAT*, an F-80C Shooting Star of the 36th Fighter Bomber Squadron/8th Fighter Bomber Group based at Suwon in February of 1952. (Fred LePage)

Beat Up Bastard was a veteran of both the Second World War and Korean missions. The B-29A flew with the 30th Bomb Squadron/19th Bomb Group during 1950. (Dick Oakley)

'Mary Lou,' an RF-80A Shooting Star of the 15th Tactical Reconnaissance Squadron/67th Tactical Reconnaissance Wing was based across the field at Kimpo from the 4th Fighter Interceptor Wing MiG Maulers during 1952. (George McKay)

Another ten ton load of 500 pound general purpose bombs is readied at Kadena Air Base, Okinawa during March of 1952, for loading aboard the *PURPLE SHAFT*, a 93rd Bomb Squadron B-29A. (USAF)

TWIN NIFTIES was another play on words describing both the twin-tailed C-119 and certain portions of the female anatomy. She belonged to the 314th Troop Carrier Group at Pusan in August of 1951. (USAF)

The pilot of this 39th Fighter Interceptor Squadron F-86E was obviously a lover of at least three ladies — *MARLINE, NANCY, and MARION*. I wonder how many more were on the port side gun bay door? (SAAF)

FOR SALE, INQUIRE WITHIN, was an RB-45C Tornado from the 91st Strategic Reconnaissance Squadron at Yokota during 1953. Even though they were jet-powered, the RB-45Cs were still easy prey for the MiGs. (AFM)

HEART'S DESIRE II was a night flying 98th Bomb Group (Medium) B-29 based out of Yokota during August of 1952. Most of the nude art work at Yokota went uncensored as opposed to the art on Kadena-based B-29s (the base commander's wife objected to the nudes). (USAF)

(Above and Below)
BEETLE BOMB, originally named after a Spike Jones song, needed something to fight for, so the 92nd Bomb Group (M) crew added a worthwhile "target" at a later date. (AFM)

SURPRISE PACKAGE, a WB-29A weather reconnaissance aircraft of the 512th RS (VLR). The 512th was based at Johnson Air Base on the northern-most Japanese island of Honshu, flying weather recon flights near the Soviet border. (USAF)

OUR L'Lass was a B-29A Superfortress that flew with the 92nd Bomb Group (Medium) during 1950. (AFM)

HOMOGENIZED ETHYL was a KB-29 tanker from the 43rd Air Refueling Squadron. The 43rd's KB-29s flew many of the first combat air-refueling missions, extending the range of bomb-laden F-84Es from the 136th Fighter Bomber Group so they could deliver their weapons on targets deep inside North Korea during 1952. (W. J. Balogh)

'PUNCH BOWL QUEEN' was a 19th Bomb Group B-29A Superfortress that was loosely named after the infamous Korean battle ground. (AFM)

HONEYBUCKET HONSHOS II was an RB-29A from the 91st Strategic Reconnaissance Squadron at Yokota Air Base, Japan. Long range reconnaissance missions against Red Chinese targets were flown by 91st RB-29s and RB-50s from the 55th SRW. (Mike Sell)

TIGER LIL was an RB-29A (42-94000) that carried some twenty-seven camera mission markings on the fuselage in Black. The aircraft was assigned to the 91st Strategic Reconnaissance Squadron. (AFM)

United Notions, a 98th Bomb Group (Medium) B-29A, was named an obvious play on words describing the forces that were fighting the communists in Korea. (AFM)

19

An unnamed F-80C of the 36th Fighter Bomber Squadron. The aircraft was staging through Kimpo Air Base during 1952, carrying the standard armament for F-80C fighter-bombers of two 500 pound GP bombs. (Warren Thompson)

This unnamed cutie adorned the side of a 35th Fighter Group F-51D Mustang in Japan during 1950. (Bob Pattison)

Beer City Special "Miss BB II," was an F-80C Shooting Star of the 36th Fighter Bomber Squadron at Suwon. The Shooting Star was flown by CAPT "Triple Tom" Owen during 1952. (Tom Owen)

THE HOLLYWOOD SPECIAL "Blow Job," was an 80th Fighter Bomber Squadron F-80C Shooting Star whose name "probably" referred to the jet's exhaust. (W. T. O'Donnell)

The Black Widow carried nose art derived from an Esquire magazine calendar. It was assigned to the 37th Bomb Squadron/17th Bomb Wing (Light) at K-1 (Pusan) during the Summer of 1952. (Robert C. Mikesh)

Ordnance for the night's mission is laid out in front of *JUNIO*, the B-26C Invader flown by COL Charles Howe when he commanded the 452nd Bomb Group (Light) at Pusan during early 1951. (John Horne)

Miss Minooki, an old sentiment resurrected from the Second World War by the crew of this 17th Bomb Wing (L) B-26C Invader based at Pusan during 1952. Her scoreboard has some 150 missions recorded as Black bomb markings. (Robert C. Mikesh)

Martha was one of the glass-nosed RB-26Cs operated by the 12th Tactical Reconnaissance Squadron/67th TRW at K-14 (Kimpo) during 1952. The Night Black RB-26Cs often flew the "Hunter" portion of "Hunter-Killer" missions along with heavily armed B-26s from the 3rd and 17th Bomb Wings (Light). (Paul Swendroski)

6th Chadwick was the sixth aircraft that MAJ Fortney of the 3rd Bomb Group (L) had flown with that name. The B-26B has only five guns fitted in the six gun nose cap with one of the center guns being removed. (Bob Esposito)

Small light planes in Korea were used in the Forward Air Controller role, commonly known as FACs. *BUNNY HOPS* was a Stinson L-5 assigned to the 8th U.S. Army during 1952. (Army)

Nancy, also known as *Honey Bucket*, was one of the Project ASHTRAY RF-86A Sabres (48-195). These aircraft had their guns removed to make room for a camera installation. The ASHTRAY RF-86As were all assigned to the 15th TRS/67th TRW at K-14. (Bill Coffey)

KATHY was an RF-86A ASHTRAY conversion. The pilot knew that *Every Man (was) A Tiger* in the 15th Tactical Reconnaissance Squadron at Kimpo. You had to be when you flew "alone, unarmed and unafraid!" (Bill Coffey)

HELLS BELLE was a B-26C from the 452nd Bomb Group (L) based at Pusan East during 1951. The 452nd Bomb Group (L) was a California Air Guard unit activated for duty in Korea. (AFM)

Bowl 'Em Over was a Meteor F.8 flown by Flying Officer Bruce Gogerly when he shot down a MiG-15. Gogerly was assigned to No 77 Squadron, Royal Australian Air Force based at K-14. (AWM)

LT Charles Wurster shot down a North Korean Yak fighter on 30 June 1950. He is talking with his crew chief next to MAID FOR ACTION, an F-80C of the 36th Fighter Bomber Squadron/8th Fighter Bomber Group, based at Itazuke AB, Japan in the Summer of 1950. (USAF)

Symon's Lemon, an RF-51D with twenty-six photo missions on its score-board. The Mustang was assigned to the 45th Tactical Reconnaissance Squadron/67th Tactical Reconnaissance Wing based at K-14 during 1952. (NAA)

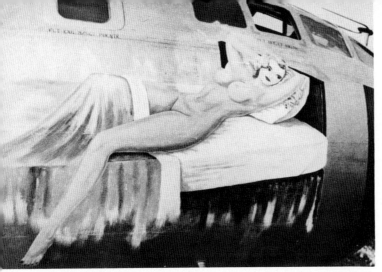

Various stages that *Never Hoppen* went through before finally being approved by the base commander's wife at Kadena. The nude was the original art work. (Dick Oakley)

SOUTH SEA SINNER was a 28th Bomb Squadron B-29A Superfortress based at Kadena Air Base, Okinawa. She was tastefully covered by her flower leis. (Dick Oakley)

When the order to cover up came through, she was given panties and a bra, but as it turned out, this still wasn't good enough to please the CO's wife. (Dick Oakley)

Persuade-Her was another B-29 painted by CAPT Dick Thompson of the 19th Bomb Group. Many of his nudes had to have clothes put on them at Kadena by order of the base commander. (Dick Oakley)

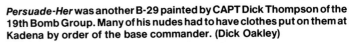

Finally, the panties and bra were exchanged for a skimpy two piece bathing suit (bikinis hadn't been invented yet) along with the complete deletion of the offensive bed. (Dick Oakley)

HOT TO GO was still another of the 19th Bomb Group B-29s based at Kadena in the Fall of 1951. The Black undersurfaces were added after the MiGs forced the B-29s to shift to night missions. (Dick Oakley)

ALL SHOOK, a B-29A of the 19th BG was named *Soft Touch* before having the undersurfaces of the aircraft painted Night Black during the Fall of 1951. (Tom Brewer)

The B-29 units seemed to have some of the best nose art in Korea. *DESTINATION KNOWN* was a B-29A of the 98th Bomb Group (M) based at Yokota, Japan. (AFM)

MULE TRAIN was a 22nd Bomb Group (M) B-29A Superfortress based at Kadena, Okinawa while on temporary assignment with the 19th Bomb Group during the Summer of 1950. (Dick Oakley)

LADY IN DIS-DRESS was a 98th Bomb Group (M) B-29A stationed at Yokota AB, Japan during 1951. (AFM)

This B-29A of the 93rd Bomb Squadron/19th Bomb Group, parked near the bomb assembly area at Kadena Air Base during 1952 was named *DIXIE BABE*. (John Shipley)

In 1955, *Dennis The Menace* was a relatively new but very popular cartoon character and the pilot of this 97th Fighter Interceptor Squadron F-86D based at Wright Patterson AFB, Ohio, must have really liked the comic strip. (AFM)

TWEETY was an F-86D Sabre Dog of the 25th Fighter Interceptor Squadron/51st Fighter Interceptor Wing based at Naha, Okinawa during 1955. The name and trim on the nose and fin was in Red. (Jack Englewright)

This 97th Fighter Interceptor Squadron F-86D Sabre Dog, based at New Castle County Airport Air Force Base, Delaware, carried the name *Joan Of Arc* and a mounted Knight during 1956. (AFM)

MI ASSAM DRAGON was carried on the side of an F-86A Sabre from the 194th Fighter Interceptor Squadron, California Air National Guard. (Jim Farmer)

First Lady Of Glasgow was a B-52D Stratofortress on display on the ramp at Edwards Air Force Base in May of 1962. That is a sailor in Dress Blues peeking into the cockpit. (Norm Taylor)

The Flying Yankees was not the personal name for this Lockheed F-94A Starfire, but rather the nickname for the Connecticut Air National Guard's 118th Fighter Interceptor Squadron based at Bradley Field. (R.W. Harrison)

The *Kentucky Rifle*, an F-86D Sabre Dog serving with the Western Air Defense Force Team at the 1956 Yuma Rocket Meet. The aircraft carries five "kill" markings for victories over the target sleeve. (NAA)

Strategic Air Command crews were rarely allowed to name their aircraft, much less put nose art on them. *City Of Winter Park* was the winner at the 1957 SAC Bombing Competition. (USAF)

Womp Bird II was an F-86D from the 39th Fighter Interceptor Squadron/51st Fighter Interceptor Wing based at Komacki Air Base, Japan during 1957. The aircraft has had a major engine overhaul and portions of the tail pipe are missing. (Merle Olmsted)

Liza Gal/El Diablo was an F-86E of the 336th FIGHTER INTERCEPTOR SQUADRON flown by CAPT Chuck Owens during 1952. The multiple names resulted from one pilot or crew chief replacing another and adding his own personal name and/or art to the aircraft without removing the previous art work. (W.K. Thomas)

Another of Karl Dittmer's 4th Fighter Interceptor Squadron F-86 Sabre works of art was LT Martin Bambrick's *WHAM BAM*. (Karl Dittmer)

One of the better artists in Korea was Karl Dittmer who painted F-86 Sabres of the 4th Fighter Interceptor Group. One of his aircraft was *GOPHER PATROL*. (Karl Dittmer)

Toni C II, was an overall Black B-26C Invader of the 34th Bomb Squadron/ 17th Bomb Wing (L) at Pusan during 1952. (Robert C. Mikesh)

Cartoon characters were still among some of the favorites for nose art subjects on fighter aircraft. *Mighty Mouse* was an F-86E-6, one of the Canadair-built Sabres assigned to the 39th Fighter Interceptor Squadron/ 51st Fighter Interceptor Wing at Suwon. (Earl Shutt)

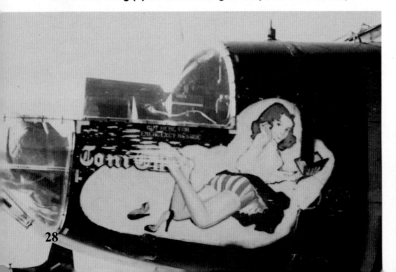

MY BABY, a B-26B from the 728th Bomb Squadron/452nd Bomb Group carries a full load of rockets and napalm on the ramp at Miho Air Base, Japan during 1951. (Robert Jackson)

The *REAM SUPREME* summed up the general attitude of every GI in a combat zone. This C-119C was from the 314th TCG. (via Warren Thompson)

I HAVE RETURNED was a B-26B from the 452nd Bomb Group at Miho Air Base, Japan. Besides the name it carried the General's famous corncob pipe. (David DeHaven)

Every theater in World War 2 had a *TOP OF THE MARK*, named after the famous San Francisco restaurant and so did Korea. This "MARK" was from the 28th Bomb Squadron/19th Bomb Group based at Kadena in 1951. (John Shipley)

SCREAM'N REBEL was an LT-6G Texan flown by CAPT Sid McNeil of the 6148th TCS at K-47, Chunchon, Korea, during 1953. (Mosquito Assn.)

The *Lucky Lady* was an F-86A Sabre flown by the "legendary" CAPT Jim Herlihy, an ace with seven kills, in one of Hollywood's "reel war" epics, "Bombers B-52." (John Campbell)

Members of the flight crew of *Spittin Kitten*, a 98th Bomb Group B-29A Superfortress, go over the preflight checklist prior to another mission against the North Koreans during 1952. (USAF)

Come On 'A My House/Our Baby was a 98th Bomb Group B-29A Superfortress based at Yokota, Japan during 1951. The name was based on a popular song of the period. (Dick Starinchak)

Miss Megook was another of CAPT Dick Thompson's B-29A Superfortress works of art that was later ordered clothed by the base commander at Kadena. (Dick Oakley)

When the order to cloth her came down from the base commander, the crew of *Miss Megook* followed that order — well almost! It is unknown what reaction the commander had to the somewhat clothed painting. (Dick Oakley)

The *DRAGON LADY* was a character in the comic strip "Terry And The Pirates" and one of the most popular names for any Far East-based aircraft in both the Second World War and Korea. This "Lady" was a 19th Bomb Group B-29A which was credited with downing five MiG-15s. (Dick Oakley)

CAPT Dick Thompson has just put the finishing touches on *Target For Tonite*, another 19th Bomb Group B-29 based at Kadena, Okinawa. Or so he thought! (Dick Oakley)

Once again, the base commander's wife objected to the nudity on the aircraft, and CAPT Thompson returned to paint clothes on his work of art. (Dick Oakley)

FOUR-A-BREAST was a B-29A Superfortress that flew with the 30th Bomb Squadron/19th Bomb Group out of Kadena, Okinawa during late 1950. (Hill)

NO SWEAT was another clothed nude from the 19th Bomb Group. The name was in Blue with Black shadow shading and the bra and panties were White. (Dick Oakley)

NOSE FOR NEWS was a Fairchild C-82 Packet used as a flying press room for reporters during the 1948 Presidential campaign. The name was in Black while the Nose was Red. (USAF)

NO SWEAT flies formation with another 19th Bomb Group Superfortress, *FOUR-A-BREAST*, over North Korea. The name on *FOUR-A-BREAST* was in Red outlined in Black. Both bombers are equipped with blind bombing radomes on the fuselage underside. (Dick Oakley)

An unnamed lady adorns the gun bay door on this 39th Fighter Interceptor Squadron F-86F Sabre at Suwon, Korea in June of 1953. (Bob Groszer)

Jo-Jo, a C-119C from the 314th TCG flew ninety-eight supply missions in Korea and was involved in all four major paratroop drops during the war. (Paul Vercammen)

Horizontal Dream was flown by CAPT John Robertson of the 80th Fighter Bomber Squadron/8th Fighter Bomber Group based at Itazuke Air Base, Japan in the Summer of 1950. (John Robertson)

What Shebolians is an unknown slang term for a well-known portion of the female anatomy, as portrayed on this B-26C from the 34th Bomb Squadron/17th Bomb Wing (L) at Pusan during 1952. (Robert C. Mikesh)

Dina Might, was an F-94B Starfire of the 4th Fighter (All Weather) Squadron based at Naha Air Base, Okinawa during 1952. Nose art on F-94s was rare. (Gerry Margraf)

MAJ T.P. Ingrassia was *THE NEW ORLEANS KID*. He flew this F-84G Thunderjet while assigned to the 111th Fighter Bomber Squadron at K-2 (Taegu) in 1951. (MAJ T.P. Ingrassia)

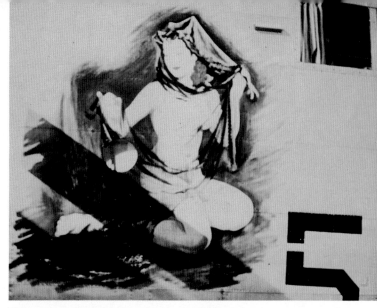

This unnamed lady on the side of a 314th Troop Carrier Group C-119C served in both Korea and Indochina during the French-Indochina War.

LT James Thompson flew *THE HUFF* and had the dragon also painted on his helmet. The dragon motif symbolized the MiG-15 that Thompson shot down on 18 May 1953, which had a large dragon painted on the fuselage. (Dean Abbott)

Karl Dittmer puts the finishing touches on *ROSIE*, an F-86E Sabre of the 335th Fighter Interceptor Squadron at K-14 during 1952. (Karl Dittmer)

One of the gaudiest Sabres in the Korean War was LT James Thompson's *THE HUFF*, of the 39th Fighter Interceptor Squadron at Suwon. The dragon was only carried on the port fuselage side. *Bill's Baby* was the marking carried on the starboard gun bay door. (D.N. Drew)

Betty Toot was a Meteor F8 of No 77 Squadron, Royal Australian Air Force based at K-14 (Kimpo) during 1952. Although primarily a ground attack unit, No 77 Squadron Meteors scored three confirmed MiG kills. (AWM)

The Spirit Of HOBO flew the 50,000th combat sortie of the Korean War. The Shooting Star was assigned to the 80th Fighter Bomber Squadron at Suwon when she set the record in October of 1952. (Zlindra via Olmsted)

This C-119C Flying Boxcar had the enviable task of delivering Marilyn Monroe to Korea during the Winter of 1952/53 and was promptly adorned with her portrait and the name *Marilyn Monroe Special*. (Richard Behilo)

NEVA HOPPEN was a B-26C Invader assigned to the 452nd Bomb Wing (Light) based at Taegu, Korea during 1951. She carries at least thirty-seven mission marks on the fuselage side. (AFM)

PEEPER was an RF-80A Shooting Star of the 15th Tactical Reconnaissance Squadron/67th Tactical Reconnaissance Wing. The RF-80A carried equipment similar to an F-80C with upgraded radios and engine. (Bill Coffey)

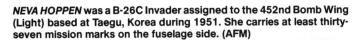

NIGHT TRAIN was an LT-6G Texan of the 6147th TCG based at Chunchon, Korea during 1953. The 6147th TCG flew Forward Air Control missions over Korea and were known as the Mosquito Squadron. (Mosquito Assn.)

Raz'N Hell was a 28th Bomb Squadron B-29A that was specially equipped to drop radio-guided RAZON bombs. These bombs were used against the Yalu River bridges near Antung in the Winter of 1950. (Dick Oakley)

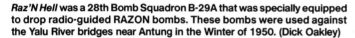

The Stinger was flown by LT Bednar of the 12th Fighter Bomber Squadron/18th Fighter Bomber Wing at Osan, Korea during 1953. MAJ Howard Ebersole is the pilot kneeling by the nose. (Howard Ebersole)

MISS "BB" III (BB stood for Big Boobs) was an F-86F Sabre fighter-bomber from the 36th Fighter Bomber Squadron/8th Fighter Bomber Wing based at Suwon during 1953. (Warren Thompson)

Sexual innuendo regarding the Japanese was still quite prevalent during the Korean War. NIP ON NEES was a 98th Bomb Group B-29A Superfortress based at Yokota, Japan. (AFM)

CREAM OF THE CROP was a 30th Bomb Squadron/19th Bomb Group B-29A based at Kadena during 1951. The aircraft was later "censored" by the base commander for being in bad taste! (Dick Oakley)

That's 'It' was one of LT Dick Thompson's best looking "pieces" of art carried by a Superfortress of the 28th Bomb Squadron/19th Bomb Group at Kadena. (Dick Oakley)

MY LOG was an AD-2 Skyraider of Marine Attack Squadron 121 (VMA-121) based at K-3 (Polang) Airfield duing 1952. The aircraft is armed with twelve 250 pound bombs and napalm tanks. (Derrickson)

This Vought F4U-5N Corsair night fighter of VC-3 was named *Yokosuka Queen*. The aircraft operated out of K-6 (Pgongtaek) Korea during July of 1953. (W. F. Geimeinhardt)

SAD SACK was a B-29A from the 22nd Bomb Group (M) that spent the Summer and Fall of 1950 on Temporary Duty (TDY) at Kadena Air Base, Okinawa. (Dick Oakley)

HOT TA GO was an overall Black RB-26C Invader from the 12th Tactical Reconnaissance Squadron/67th Tactical Reconnaissance Wing based at Kimpo during 1952. (Dick Starinchak)

Mickey's dog *Pluto* has his sights set on a MiG-15 as his next meal. *Pluto* was an F-86E Sabre of the 25th Fighter Interceptor Squadron at K-13 during 1953. (Dick Geiger)

Now that's real "nose" art. This F-86E Sabre was from the 16th Fighter Interceptor Squadron, based at Suwon, Korea during 1953. (Frank Tomlinson)

DENNIS THE MENACE asks the Chinese Reds if they *Wanna Play?*. LT L. R. Ivins flew this F-86F fighter-bomber while attached to the 67th Fighter Bomber Squadron based at K-55 (Osan) in November of 1953. (Bernard Kibort)

KIMPO KAT was a C-119C of the 314th TCG that participated in all the major parachute operations in the Korean War, including the 187th REGIMENTAL COMBAT TEAM drop into Sunchon on 30 December 1950. (Paul Vercammen)

Beetle Bum was a T-6D Texan that ran into accurate flak over North Korea. The "Bum" flew with the famous Mosquito Squadron, the 6147th Tactical Air Control Group during 1950. (Mosquito Assn.)

BUZZY McGOO II, an F-84G assigned to the 7th Fighter Bomber Squadron/49th Fighter Bomber Group at K-2, also had two *LADIES WILD* on the fuselage. (Thomas Washburn)

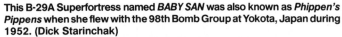

CHIEF MAC'S 10 LITTLE INDIANS was carried on a B-29A Superfortress of the 98th Bomb Group based at Yokota during 1950. (AFM)

CREAM OF THE CROP shows how some of the crews felt about their art work being censored. When ordered to cover up, they just slapped a sign over her offending areas. (Dick Oakley)

This B-29A Superfortress named *BABY SAN* was also known as *Phippen's Pippens* when she flew with the 98th Bomb Group at Yokota, Japan during 1952. (Dick Starinchak)

This B-29A Superfortress named *THE WILD GOOSE* flew with the 92nd Bomb Group out of Yokota in the Fall of 1950. (AFM)

Toddlin' Turtle flew with the 22nd Bomb Group at Kadena in the Fall of 1950. The 22nd Bomb Group was one of the B-29s units rushed to the Korean Theater in the Summer of 1950. (Dick Oakley)

WHERE NEXT?, a 98th Bomb Group B-29A Superfortress, has had a long and distinguished career and she seems ready for more. The aircraft and crew served in both Europe and the Pacific. (AFM)

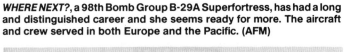

This B-29A Superfortress, named *Myasis Dragon,* was transferred from the 92nd Bomb Group at Yokota, Japan to the "censored" 19th Bomb Group at Kadena, Okinawa. (Dick Oakley)

On arrival in Kadena, *Myasis Dragon* promptly had the name altered to meet the rules set up by the base commander at Kadena. The crew simply overpainted the offending word with White paint. (Dick Oakley)

This B-29A named *DOUBLE OR NUTHIN'* flew with the 19th Bomb Group at Kadena. The painted on window behind the name holds the face of a crewman who hasn't seen many women lately. (Hill)

B-29A side number 6361 was a *LONELY LADY.* She flew with the 98th Bomb Group at Yokota, Japan during 1951. (AFM)

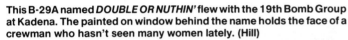

Miss Jackie The Rebel was still another prime example of CAPT Dick Thompson's gorgeous ladies being forced to dress before going off to war. The rebel lady was given a rebel flag bathing suit top to please the CO's wife. (Hill)

The *LAKE SUCCESS EXPRESS*, A B-29A of the 92nd Bomb Group during the Summer of 1950 had the names of the crews girl friends/wives painted by the crewman's position. The 92nd Bomb Group had been based at Spokane Field before being sent to Korea. (AFM)

BATTY BETTY II was a modified Lockheed F-5G Lightning flown by Jack Hardwick (also known as "the Madman Muntz Of The Air") at the 1948 National Air Race held at Cleveland Municipal Airport. (Charles Trask via Dave McLaren)

ACE IN THE HOLE was an F-94B Starfire of the 319th F(AW)S that was based at K-13. The unit had detachments throughout South Korea for night air defense. The 'Ace' was parked on the ramp at Taegu during June 1953. (Alan Fine)

SWEET MUDDER was an F-86L Sabre of the 329th Fighter Interceptor Squadron based at George Air Force Base, California during 1958. (Marty Isham)

Personalized aircraft were rare in the Strategic Air Command, and even fewer carried nose art. *Old Blue*, was a B-47E Stratojet of the 310th Bomb Wing based at MacDill Air Force Base, Florida. (USAF)

The nose art predates the cartoon character, but it shows how the crews felt about the performance of the F-86D Sabre. *RoadRunner* was from the 97th Fighter Interceptor Squadron at Wright Patterson AFB during the late 1950s. (D.N. Drew)

The Tender Trap was named after a Frank Sinatra movie and song title. It was one of the B-52Bs that participated in five live-fire nuclear tests at Enewetok Atoll during the mid-1950s. (AFM)

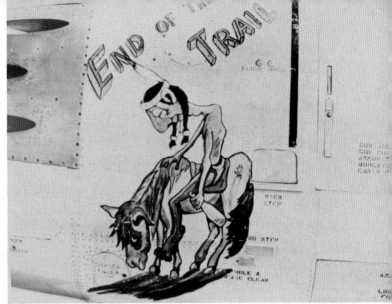

End Of The Trail indicated that this F-86A Sabre of the 194th Fighter Interceptor Squadron/California Air National Guard was probably the last stop before the bone yard. (Jim Farmer)

Ground crews perform maintenance on one of the engines of the LUCKY LADY II. This 8th Air Force B-50A made an around the world record flight during 1950. (AFM)

Boards shares the ramp with other F-86As of the 194th Fighter Interceptor Squadron at Fresno, California in 1953. Most of California Air National Guard F-86As carried nose art in one form or another during this period. (Jim Farmer)

41

This F-80C Shooting Star, named *RAMBLIN-RECK-TEW*, was flown by LT Robert Dewald when he shot down a North Korean IL-10 during July of 1950. The aircraft carried a small North Korean star under the cockpit. (Robert Dewald)

This unnamed nude was painted on the side of an F-84G Thunderjet from the 58th Fighter Bomber Group at Taegu, Korea during 1952. (David W. Menard)

Bugs' (ball) Buster conveyed the attitude of the Superfortress crews that flew the missions into MiG Alley. These were "ball buster missions" that cost a lot of B-29s. Bugs flew with the 28th Bomb Squadron. (Dick Oakley)

THE WILD MOOOSE was a C-119C Flying Boxcar of the 61st Troop Carrier Squadron, known as The Green Hornets. The squadron was based at Taegu during the Summer of 1951. (Paul Vercammen)

OVER EXPOSED was a 91st Strategic Reconnaissance Squadron RB-29A based at Yokota. The 91st SRS was responsible for all Air Force long range reconnaissance missions flown during the Korean War. (Dick Oakley)

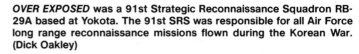

"JOHNS OTHER WIFE" was his B-29A. The Superfortress was assigned to the 19th Bomb Group in 1952. Quite a difference between this "lady" and those done by CAPT Dick Thompson. (John Shipley)

DOWN'S CLOWNS was a 92nd Bomb Group B-29A Superfortress that was later shot down by North Korean MiG-15 fighters during 1951. (John Rusch)

COMMAND DECISION is easily the most famous B-29 from the Korean War. The crew of this 28th Bomb Squadron B-29 shot down five MiG-15 jet fighters in 1950/51. Its fuselage has been preserved and exhibited at the Air Force Museum in Dayton, Ohio. (USAF)

THE OUTLAW was a 28th Bomb Squadron B-29A named for the Howard Hughes movie. The likeness of Jane Russell, who starred in the movie, was taken from the movie posters that came out with the film. (Dick Oakley)

LI'L DOTTIE was flown by LT Roy Marsh while assigned to the 80th Fighter Bomber Squadron/8th Fighter Bomber Group when he shot down a North Korean Il-10 on 29 June 1950. (Warren Thompson)

The *JOLLEY ROGER* was the personal aircraft of CAPT Clifford Jolley, one of the "MiG Hunters" of the 4th Fighter Interceptor Wing at Kimpo. Jolley shot down seven MiGs during 1952. (Clifford Jolley)

KTTV CHANNEL 11 was one of the radar-busting B-26Bs from the 452nd Bomb Group at Taegu. It was named after a Los Angeles television station that went to Korea to cover the California Reserve unit. (David Dehaven)

Dorothy L/PANTHER QUEEN was an F-80C of the 16th Fighter Interceptor Squadron/51st Fighter Interceptor Group based at K-13 (Suwon) in 1951. The Shooting Star was equipped with long range "Misawa" drop tanks specially designed for combat in Korea. (R.F. Wehr)

HONEYBUCKET was one of eleven F-86A Sabres that were converted to RF-86A under Project ASHTRAY. The "Bucket" was assigned to the 15th Tactical Reconnaissance Squadron/67th Tactical Reconnaissance Wing at Kimpo during 1952. This was the only RF-86A lost in Korea. (Robert Lamprecht)

SQUEEZE PLAY was a B-29A Superfortress assigned to the 92nd Bomb Group in the Fall of 1950. It was a play on an old military saying for being in BIG trouble — "catching your tit in a wringer." (AFM)

The 452nd Bomb Group was a California Air Force Reserve unit that was activated for the Korean War. Many of their aircraft had names relating to their home state. *Hollywood HANGOVER* was from the 728th Bomb Squadron. (Robert Jackson)

Dagmar and Muchie were a pair of VF-54 AD-4 Skyraiders aboard USS ESSEX during the Fall of 1951. *Dagmar* was a very voluptuous blonde television personality in the early 1950s. (V.A. Fleming)

BUBBA BOY, a B-47E Stratojet of the 4925th Test Group (Atomic) following one of the Atomic missions against Enewetok during 1956. (AFM)

THE TURTLE was also known as *Truculent Turtle*. The P2V-1 Neptune flew non-stop from Perth, Australia to Columbus, Ohio setting a new distance record. The aircraft visited the Cleveland National Air Show during November 1946. (Ron Picciani)

(Above And Below)
The crew of *Mean Hairy Hawg* pose in front of their North American AJ-2P Savage reconnaissance bomber (side number PB 6). The aircraft was assigned to Detachment Queen 3 of Heavy Photographic Squadron Sixty-One (VJ-61), home based at Naval Air Facility Sangley Point on the island of Luzon in the Republic of the Philippines during May of 1954. The small emblem behind the White hawg is the unit insignia of VJ-61 which was later redesignated as VAP-61. (V.A. Fleming)

LT A.J. Norris in front of his North American AJ-2P reconnaissance patrol bomber from Heavy Photographic Squadron Sixty One (VJ-61) based at NAF Sangley Point on Luzon during 1954. Art on land-based Navy aircraft, while rare, was far more common than on carrier aircraft. (V.A. Fleming)

Smoky JOE was an overall Natural Metal Lockheed U-2A high altitude air sampling aircraft based at Edwards Air Force Base during the early 1960s. (John Andrews)

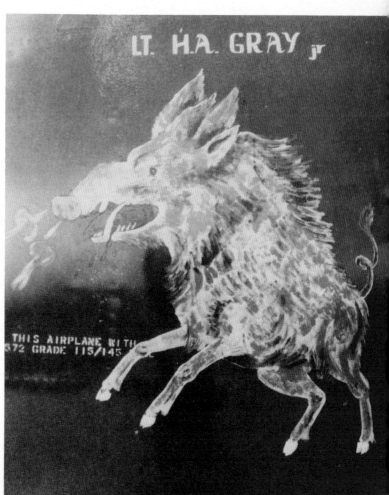

Mechanics conduct a complete overhaul of this 1st Marine Air Wing F9F-2 Panther at Pohang, Korea during June of 1951. The Panther has a panther "face" and claws in White on the nose. (USMC)

FATHER DAN was a sharkmouthed F-86E Sabre of the 25th Fighter Interceptor Squadron that was named after the Chaplin of the 51st Fighter Interceptor Group at K-13. (George Howell)

Miss Tena was flown by COL Woodrow Wilmot when he commanded the 8th Fighter Bomber Wing at Suwon in 1953. The tail and nose command stripes on the F-86F-30 fighter-bomber are Blue, Yellow and Red. (Don Garrett, Jr.)

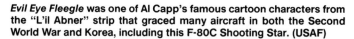

LT Harvey Brown flew this F-86F Sabre fighter-bomber with the 67th Fighter Bomber Squadron at Osan, Korea during the Summer of 1953. The artwork was painted on by his crew chief. (Harvey Brown)

My Mimi, was an RF-51D Mustang of the 45th Tactical Reconnaissance Squadron (known as the Polka Dot Squadron). The unit flew recon missions over the front and along the North Korean road net during 1951. (USAF)

Evil Eye Fleegle was one of Al Capp's famous cartoon characters from the "L'il Abner" strip that graced many aircraft in both the Second World War and Korea, including this F-80C Shooting Star. (USAF)

Marine MAJ John Glenn (later Astronaut and Congressman) was the *MiG Mad Marine*. He shot down three MiG-15s during 1953 while on temporary assignment with the 25th Fighter Interceptor Squadron at Suwon. (COL Robert Baldwin)

BROWN NOSE was a 452nd Bomb Wing (Light) B-26B Invader. The aircraft flew the unit's 10,000th sortie in December of 1951. The ground crew, SGT Raymond Severy, SGT Raymond Lowther and SGT Thomas Meer were congratulated on the occasion by MAJ Gilbert Nevling. (USAF)

Betty Jane was a gunfighting "lady" with the 45th Tactical Reconnaissance Squadron at K-14 during 1952. The polka dot prop spinner was a symbol of the 45th Tactical Reconnaissance Squadron. The name was in Red with a White outline. (Dave Colbert)

After a complaint from the base commander's wife at Kadena Air Base, all the 19th Bomb Group B-29As were forced to put clothes on all the nude art work. *Southern Comfort* from the 30th Bomb Squadron was given a two piece swim suit. (Dick Oakley)

This 98th Bomb Group (Medium) B-29A Superfortress carried a slightly different variation on the "Terry And The Pirates" *Dragon Lady* character during 1951. (AFM)

Cat Girl, a 28th Bomb Squadron B-29A at Kadena during late 1952. She had started out nude on a Natural Metal B-29; now she has had both the night camouflage and clothes added to the original art. (AFM)

Armament specialists work on the upper turret of *TO EACH HIS OWN*, a B-29A Superfortress that flew with the 98th Bomb Group out of Yokota, Japan during 1951. (AFM)

This B-29A, named *LUCKY DOG*, flew missions out of Kadena with the 93rd Bomb Squadron during 1950. (Dick Oakley)

Dead Jug was a 93rd Bomb Squadron B-29A. The name was in reference to the trouble-plagued Pratt and Whitney R-3350 power plants used on the Boeing Superfortress. (Dick Oakley)

HOT TO GO was the attitude that most of the 98th Bomb Group (Medium) crews had during that first Summer of 1950. At that time everyone had the feeling that the war would be over by Christmas. (AFM)

NO SWEAT has had a pair of strategically placed "ear muffs" painted on after the censorship edict went into effect at Kadena. (Hill)

BIG SHMOO was a 93rd Bomb Squadron/19th Bomb Group B-29A based at Kadena. The Shmoo was another one of the characters in Al Capp's cartoon strip "L'il Abner." The band around the nose and the nosewheel door are Red. (Dick Oakley)

Peacemaker, was a B-29A Superfortress of the 22nd Bomb Group, which shared the field at Kadena with the 19th Bomb Group. (Dick Oakley)

Star Duster was another Black-bellied 30th Bomb Squadron B-29A Superfortress on the ramp at Kadena during 1952. The nosewheel has a painted on whitewall tire. (John Shipley)

OUR GAL was one of LT Dick Thompson's best pieces of art. He added a polka dot bathing suit when the word was passed down to clothe the girls. The nose band was in Red. (Dick Oakley)

The Old Man was the F-86F Sabre flown by the commander of the 8th Fighter Bomber Group at K-13 in the Summer of 1953. The various types of weapons that the F-86F was capable of carrying were laid out in front of the aircraft for a press display. (NAA)

CAPT Richard Chandler scratches the tail of *Sylvester*, an RF-86A ASH-TRAY aircraft. *Sylvester* is reading the instructions on *How To Use Your Brownie*, which referred to the cameras installed in the RF-86A at K-14 in 1952. (USAF)

Little Mike, flown by CAPT Robinson Risner, had Bugs Bunny checking out a discharge paper painted on the starboard side of the F-86E Sabre along with four Red star kill markings on the gun bay door. (Robert Lamprecht)

Bills Baby/Miss Jerry was the artwork carried on the opposite side of LT James Thompson's *The Huff*. T/SGT Bill Manney was the crew chief on *The Huff* and his personal markings were carried on the starboard gun bay door. (Bill Manney)

Art on the Sabres in Korea ran from gorgeous nudes to ridiculous cartoons like *MIKE'S BIRD*, an F-86F Sabre with the 39th Fighter Interceptor Squadron at K-13 during 1953. (Bob Groszer)

The Fickle Finger, a 136th Fighter Bomber Group F-84G Thunderjet, was typical of the attitude of the crews and GIs in Korea as the war dragged on with no end, let alone victory, in sight.

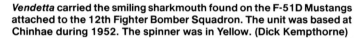

Vendetta carried the smiling sharkmouth found on the F-51D Mustangs attached to the 12th Fighter Bomber Squadron. The unit was based at Chinhae during 1952. The spinner was in Yellow. (Dick Kempthorne)

MIDNITE SINNER was a 68th Fighter (All Weather) Squadron F-82G based at Itazuke AB, Japan. The 68th had detachments throughout Japan and South Korea and were responsible for intercepting the North Korean PO-2 Bedcheck Charlies that harassed UN bases every night. (Don Garrett, Jr.)

The famous *Monie* was Robert Mikesh's B-26C Invader when he flew with the 37th Bomb Squadron/17th Bomb Wing (Light Night Attack) based at Pusan in the Fall of 1952. (Robert C. Mikesh)

THE THING, a 61st Troop Carrier Squadron (Green Hornets) C-119C Flying Boxcar based at Taegu in 1951, was named for the classic horror movie, "The Thing." (Paul Vercammen)

BUGS II, a 17th Bomb Wing (Light) B-26C Invader based at K-3 (Pusan) during 1952, used the famous rabbit as its mascot. (AFM)

SHOOT YOU'RE FADED, the venerable crapshooter's term was carried over from the Second World War and painted on this 36th Fighter Bomber Squadron/8th Fighter Bomber Group F-80C based at K-2 during 1951. (USAF)

HARD'S HORNET, an F-86F Sabre fighter-bomber from the 67th Fighter Bomber Squadron/18th Fighter Bomber Group, was flown by LT Robert Hard in June of 1953. (Warren Thompson)

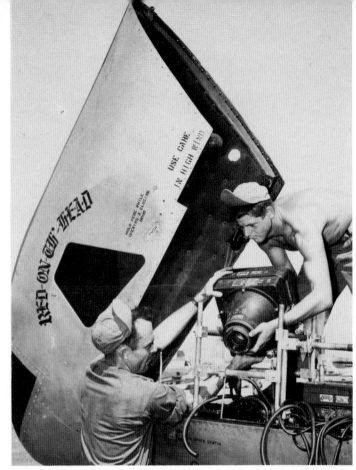

SGT Harry Hanst and CPL Peter Grant install a loaded K-24 camera into the camera bay of *Red-On-Th'-Head*, an RF-80A Shooting Star of the 8th Tactical Reconnaissance Squadron based at Yokota during the Summer of 1950. (USAF)

PUDDY TAT was a fighter-bomber F-86F Sabre with the 12th Fighter Bomber Squadron/18th Fighter Bomber Wing based at K-55 in 1953. The 18th Fighter Bomber Group transitioned from F-51Ds to F-86Fs in the Spring of 1953. (Dick Kempthorne)

LT Dick Thompson starts filling in the body on *That's 'It'*, a Red banded 93rd Bomb Squadron B-29A at Kadena, Okinawa. The original artwork on the Superfortress was nude. (Tom Brewer)

Miss Spokane, a 92nd Bomb Group B-29A on temporary duty to Yokota, carried ten mission markings under the cockpit. The artwork was copied from a photo of the real Miss Spokane of 1950 that had been sent to the group from the Spokane Chamber of Commerce. (Boeing)

STOVE PIPE SUE was one of the armed T-33A Shooting Stars assigned to the 51st Fighter Interceptor Group at K-13 in 1952. Every jet group in Korea had several armed T-33As that were used as hack aircraft and airborne command posts. (Oscar Lind)

Later *That's 'It'* had a flimsy nightgown added to the painting. The artist's signature is visible just to the right of the figure. (Dick Oakley)

Soft Touch was another B-29A Superfortress from the 28th Bomb Squadron/19th Bomb Group at Kadena. (Hill)

"Run 'em back north over the 38th Parallel" was the typical sentiment of the bomber crews at Kadena during 1950. *MISSION INN* flew with the 22nd Bomb Group. (USAF)

Some Superforts carried art in other locations than the nose. This is an example of "tail art." *HOLTON'S BAR'L* was a description of the tail gunner's "office" on this 92nd Bomb Group B-29A at Yokota. (Wayne)

ISLAND QUEEN was another example of Dick Thompson's art work on a 28th Bomb Squadron B-29A. The nose band and nosewheel door were in Dark Green. (Dick Oakley)

ROUGH ROMAN was a 28th Bomb Squadron B-29A Superfortress at Kadena during 1951. (Tom Brewer)

SHEEZA GOER flew with the 30th Bomb Squadron at Kadena. The 19th Bomb Group based at Kadena, Okinawa flew combat missions over the course of the entire Korean War. (Dick Oakley)

Mac's Effort, a 92nd Bomb Group(M) B-29A Superfortress, carried a double entendre name derived from the Air Force term for an all-out attack. (AFM)

LUCIFER was one of the specially modified 19th Bomb Group B-29As that carried the radio-guided 12,000 pound TARZON bomb against the Yalu River bridges. (AFM)

JITA stood for "Jab In The Ass." The Black bellied B-29A Superfortress flew with the 30th Bomb Squadron/19th Bomb Group during 1951. (Dick Oakley)

The Bluetailfly flew with the Blue-tailed 30th Bomb Squadron at Kadena during 1950. The B-29s of the 30th BS carried a Blue band on the nose and across the vertical fin. (Dick Oakley)

Sure Thing was a 19th Bomb Group B-29A that had a very low cut blouse and hiked up skirt painted over her original nude art. (Hill)

ROCK HAPPY was a 93rd Bomb Squadron B-29A named for the GI slang reference for Okinawa - The Rock. This B-29 flew over seventy-five combat missions over Korea. (USAF)

"Stateside Reject" from the 19th Bomb Group in 1951. Throughout the war, the 19th Bomb Group had fine artists for their B-29 "canvas." (Dick Oakley)

TARHEEL STATE, a 22nd Troop Carrier Squadron C-54, delivered bombs and fuzes to the fighter units at Kimpo after the base was recaptured in September of 1950. (USAF)

Sweet Miss Lillian, a 37th Bomb Squadron B-26C Invader based at K-1 (Pusan) in the Fall of 1952. The art was based on a Vargas girl seen on a 1952 Esquire calendar. (Robert C. Mikesh)

The Golden Bear, a 17th Bomb Wing(LNA) B-26C on the Pusan ramp in June of 1953. The all-Black B-26s of the 17th and 3rd Bomb Wing flew night intruder missions along the North Korean road net, usually in Hunter-Killer teams with another B-26. (USAF)

DOT and *Mary Lou* sit in one of the sandbag revetments used by 15th Tactical Reconnaissance Squadron RF-80s at K-14 during 1952. *Mary Lou*, an RF-80A, has over 100 photo missions, while *DOT* was one of the newer RF-80Cs. (George McKay)

OLIE was the personal F-84G Thunderjet of COL Joe Davis, Jr., Commander of the 58th Fighter Bomber Group at K-8 in 1953. The buzz number on the aircraft's side had Red shadow shading. (Don Garrett, Jr.)

Ricki-Ticki sits on the Taegu ramp with other 314th Troop Carrier Group C-119C Flying Boxcars loaded with supplies for the troops along the front in August of 1951. (USAF)

MAJ Elbert Kerstetter leans on the drop tank of *HONEST JOHN*, an F-86E Sabre with the 336th Fighter Interceptor Squadron/4th Fighter Interceptor Wing at K-14 during September of 1952. (USAF)

SGT George Hale of the Royal Australian Air Force touches the map of home on *'Halestorm,'* a Meteor Mk 8 of No 77 Squadron, RAAF at K-14. The words "MiG Killer" were written in the gun dust — a very rare occurrence for the Meteors. (AWM)

KIPED/COCHISE was an F-86E Sabre of the 335th Fighter Interceptor Squadron at K-14 during 1952. *KIPED* has a train with twelve rail cars, six trucks and one MiG to its credit. (Ken Buchanen)

DAIJOBU was previously named *Moon's Moonbeam*. She was a RB-29A Superfortress assigned to the 91st SRS at Yokota, Japan during 1952. (Dick Starinchak)

Big Mike and *Bears Bite* share the ramp at Larson Air Force Base with other F-104A Starfighters from the 538th Fighter Interceptor Squadron in 1957. They are armed with Sidewinder air-to-air missiles on the wingtip rails. (Marty Isham)

Tail art was rare at any time, but even more so on post Second World War aircraft. This tiger was all saddled up and ready to go on this 26th Fighter Interceptor Squadron F-86D based at Clark Air Base, Republic of the Philippines. (Merle Olmsted)

Most people generally associate Playboy magazine nose art with the Vietnam era but it actually got started in the early 1950s. This 4th Fighter Interceptor Squadron F-86D had the Playboy Bunny emblem painted on the nose when it was based at Misawa Air Base, Japan during 1959. (Tom Brewer)

Ole 1404 was certainly not a turtle of any kind, since it set the World Absolute Speed Record at 1404 mph while assigned to the 538th Fighter Interceptor Squadron at Larson AFB, Washington. (Don Dickman)

CAPT Howard Curran flew 105 missions in his F-80C Shooting Star which was named *Kansas Tornado*. CAPT Curran was attached to the 16th Fighter Interceptor Squadron at K-13 in July of 1951. (USAF)

Temptation was a 4th Fighter Interceptor Group F-86E based at Kimpo that had Marilyn Monroe's Playboy magazine calendar spread painted on the nose. (W.P. Dunbar)

Dream Girl, a 17th Bomb Wing (Light Night Attack) B-26C based at K-2 (Pusan) during 1952. These markings are preserved on the B-26C that is on display at the Air Force Museum in Dayton, Ohio. (Robert C. Mikesh)

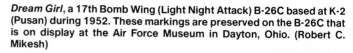

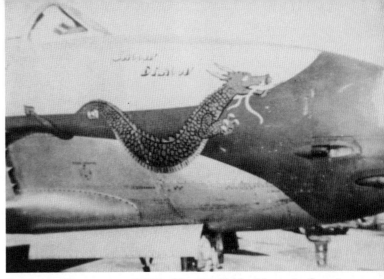

CPL James Hantelman wipes off the gun dust residue from the nose of *SEDUCTIVE SHIRLEY*, an F-80C Shooting Star of the 25th Fighter Interceptor Squadron at Suwon in December of 1950. Most of the nose 'art' on fighter aircraft in Korea was simply a name. (USAF)

The *Saggin' Dragon* was an F-80C of the 16th Fighter Interceptor Squadron that came to grief when it made a wheels-up landing at K-13 during 1951. (David W. Menard)

LT Simon Anderson stands next to *Hot To Trot*, an F-86E Sabre of the 25th Fighter Interceptor Squadron at K-13. LT Anderson shot down two MiG-15s in September 1952 and his kill markings were painted on the side of the Sabre next to the name. (Simon K. Anderson)

Wini was a Cessna L-19 Bird Dog from 8th U.S. Army Corps Headquarters at Seoul City in 1951. The nose is Red and White and an 8th Corps patch was carried on the vertical fin. (Robert Esposito)

The old crap-shooting expression, *SHOOT YOU'RE FADED*, was used as often in the Korean War as it was in the Second World War. This time it was on an F-51D Mustang from the 35th Fighter Interceptor Group based at Pusan during December 1950. (USAF)

O'L ANCHOR ASS was flown by MAJ William O'Donnell when he was the commander of the 36th Fighter Bomber Squadron flying out of Kimpo in the Summer of 1951. (William O'Donnell)

Although artwork on C-119s was very plentiful and quite colorful, nose art on other cargo types was usually a simple name. *HONEYMOONER'S SPECIAL* was a C-46 that got stuck in the mud at K-13 and to be pushed out manually by Korean laborers! (USAF)

The growling tiger was typical of the attitude of 5th Fighter Command pilots in Korea. This was especially true in Tiger Flight of the 25th Fighter Interceptor Squadron at Suwon in the Spring of 1951, in spite of the fact that they were at a distinct disadvantage with the MiGs. (Tom Foote)

As in the Second World War, Walt Disney characters were often used as nose art during the Korean War. *L'il Bambi* was flown by LT George Dean of the 68th F(AW)S based at Itazuke, Japan during July of 1950. (George Dean)

A fitting conclusion to this volume has to be this B-29A Superfortress named *Fujigmo*, which meant (cleaned up) "Forget You Jack, I Got My Orders." This was the magic saying that meant it was time to go home and start living again. (Dick Oakley)